# The Shoemaker and the Elves

☙ retold by Leni Smith Covington ☙
illustrated by Taylor B. Randolph

KENYON AVENUE PRESS
Durham, North Carolina

*The Shoemaker and the Elves*
ISBN: 978-1-7366593-0-4 softcover
ISBN: 978-1-7366593-1-1 ebook
Library of Congress Control Number: 2021904462

Copyright ©2021 by Leni Smith Covington
All Rights Reserved.

No part of this book may be reproduced in any written, electronic, recording, or photocopy form without the prior written permission of the publisher, except for the inclusion of brief quotations in a review.

Publisher's Cataloging-in-Publication data

Names: Covington, Leni Smith, author. | Randolph, Taylor B., illustrator.
Title: The shoemaker and the elves / retold by Leni Smith Covington; illustrated by Taylor B. Randolph.
Description: Durham, NC: Kenyon Avenue Press, 2021. | Summary: A poor shoemaker and his wife become successful with the help of two elves who finish his shoes during the night. His wife joins him in the business by knitting socks. They share their money with others who need it.
Identifiers: LCCN: 2021904462 | ISBN: 978-1-7366593-0-4 (paperback) | 978-1-7366593-1-1 (ebook)
Subjects: LCSH Elves--Juvenile fiction. | Fairy tales. | Folklore. | BISAC JUVENILE FICTION / Fairy Tales & Folklore / Adaptations
Classification: LCC PZ7.1.C686 Sh 2021 | DDC 398.2--dc23

Illustrations by Taylor B. Randolph
Copyedited by Lucy Long Ivey
Book Design by Bob Schram, Bookends Design

Printed in the United States of America

Published by
KENYON AVENUE PRESS
Durham, NC

kenyonavenuepress.com • info@kenyonavenuepress.com

# Dedicated to

*Gerda Gwendolyn Kott*
*Eurythmist, Teacher, Friend*

*To teachers, students of all ages learning to read,*
*and all of you who read this book aloud*

Once upon a time, there lived a shoemaker and his wife. They dwelt in a very small home. The shoemaker had nothing but a small piece of leather left with which to make one pair of shoes. He and his wife were so poor that they had only enough food left for one small meal.

So the shoemaker cut out the leather for the shoes and put it on the worktable. It was late, and the sun was setting in the sky. It was getting dark. The shoemaker decided to work on the shoes the next morning.

The shoemaker and his wife ate the last of their food and got themselves ready for bed. They said their evening prayers and were soon fast asleep.

When the shoemaker awoke the next morning, he said his morning prayers. He went to his worktable to begin to make a pair of shoes from the leather he had cut out the evening before. Much to his surprise, the leather had already been sewn into a new pair of shoes! "My goodness, how did this happen?" wondered the shoemaker. "These shoes are perfect! The stitching is perfect!"

The shoemaker put these fancy shoes in the window of his shop to sell. The shoes were so handsome! Soon a buyer came along and bought the shoes.

The buyer was so pleased with the shoes that he paid more than usual for them.

The shoemaker and his wife now had enough money to buy more food and enough leather for two pairs of shoes.

The shoemaker went to the leather shop and bought the leather for those two pairs of shoes. Once again, the shoemaker cut out the leather when he returned home. Now, the sun was setting, and it was growing dark. So he left the leather on the worktable so that he could make the two pairs of shoes the next morning.

The shoemaker and his wife ate their evening meal and got themselves ready for bed. They said their evening prayers and were soon fast asleep. When the shoemaker woke up, he went to the worktable to begin to make new shoes. Much to his surprise, the leather had been sewn into two new pairs of shoes!

The shoemaker put these shoes in the window of his shop to sell. Soon two buyers came, and each one bought a pair of shoes. The buyers gave him so much money that he had enough money for even more leather and plenty of food.

The shoemaker went to the leather shop and bought enough leather for four pairs of shoes. When he got home, he cut out the leather to make new shoes and laid it on the worktable. Once again, as the sun began to set and it grew dark, he left the leather on the worktable so that he could make the four pairs of shoes the next morning.

The shoemaker and his wife ate their evening meal and got themselves ready for bed. They said their evening prayers and were soon fast asleep. When they awoke the next morning, *four* pairs of shoes had been made.

And so it went. The shoemaker would cut out leather for new shoes and lay it on his worktable each evening. In the morning when the shoemaker awoke, he would be surprised with new shoes that had been sewn and were ready to be sold. Soon the shoemaker was making so much money from the shoes that he became rich.

One evening just before St. Nicholas Day, the shoemaker was cutting out leather for shoes to make the next day. He said to his wife, "What if we stayed awake tonight and tried to find out who is helping us?"

His wife thought this was a very good idea. It was almost midnight. The wife lit a candle in the dark. The shoemaker and his wife hid behind some clothes that were hanging from pegs on the wall. They kept a lookout.

Exactly at midnight, two tiny little men came into the house. They were wearing very thin and raggedy clothes and no shoes at all. They sat down at the workbench. They began to work, their tiny hands and fingers punching and sewing and hammering with such skill! The shoemaker stared in amazement with wide eyes and an open mouth. How could this be? How could those tiny little men work so well with those tiny little fingers on those tiny little hands?

The tiny men sang a song to the rhythm of their stitching:

*I stitch, I stitch,*
*I stitch away.*
*I stitch and stitch*
*I make new shoes today!*

They sang joyfully while they worked. They did not stop working until they had finished making shoes with all the leather the shoemaker had cut out. They put the shoes on the worktable. Then they jumped up and ran off in a flash.

The next morning, the shoemaker's wife said, "Those little men have worked hard for us. We must find a way to show our gratitude. They must get cold, running around with so little to keep them warm. What if I sewed them some little coats and shirts and vests and trousers? And I could knit them some socks and hats, too. You could make them each a pair of shoes."

The shoemaker said, "That sounds like a good idea to me." He and his wife worked all day long on this project. In the evening, they wrapped the presents. Instead of putting the leather cut out for shoes on the worktable, they left the presents there. Once again, the wife lit a candle, and they hid behind the clothes hanging from pegs on the wall. They wanted to see how the little men would react.

At midnight, the two tiny little men scampered in and were ready to start to stitch and hammer. But there was no leather cut out on the table. In its place were little packages, all wrapped. The little men were puzzled. When they opened the packages, they were so happy!

They put on their beautiful new clothes and began to dance in a ring and sing:

> *Ting-a-ling-a-ling,*
> *Bells do ring.*
> *Ting-a-ling-a-ling,*
> *We do sing.*
> *Ting-a-ling-a-ling,*
> *We dance in a ring,*
> *We thank you for the gifts*
> *you did bring!*

They skipped and danced and jumped over chairs and benches. At last, they danced out the door and were never seen again.

The shoemaker and his wife were delighted to have seen the little elves so happy. The shoemaker continued to find joy in making shoes for the rest of his life. The shoemaker's wife eagerly knit socks to sell side by side with the shoes. They continued to make money and to share their money with others who needed it. The shoemaker and his wife were happy and successful with whatever they tried to do in this world.

I stitch, I stitch,
I stitch away.
I stitch and stitch
I make new shoes today!

Ting-a-ling-a-ling,
Bells do ring.
Ting-a-ling-a-ling,
We do sing.
Ting-a-ling-a-ling,
We dance in a ring,
We thank you for the gifts
you did bring!

## About the Author

LENI SMITH COVINGTON has been both a Waldorf teacher and a public school teacher for 30-plus years. She has taught Infant Education through Grade 5 as a classroom teacher, both in-class and homebound, and as a teacher of special-education, reading-resource, and English-language learners. She founded two private Waldorf preschools and has mentored Waldorf teachers in Xian, China, and Raleigh, North Carolina. She has two sons, and five grandchildren whom she loves reading aloud to.

## About the Illustrator

TAYLOR B. RANDOLPH worked as a medical and natural science illustrator in Germany and the United States for 10 years. She subsequently worked as a substitute teacher at the Charlottesville Waldorf School in Charlottesville, Virginia, where she currently resides with her husband.

# Advance Praise for The Shoemaker and the Elves

*This picture book was such a delight! I have fond memories of fairy tales'
being read to me when I was a child, and, as a second-grade teacher,
I still use these fairy tales for teaching children to find the central message,
which they can usually readily grasp in these timeless tales.
The central message of this book teaches how to persevere and to be proud of one's
blessings, no matter how small. The shoemaker and his wife are models of hard work
and persistence. The way these two characters work together to build success
is both admirable and heartwarming.
The many lessons to take from this retelling of* The Shoemaker and the Elves *are
still powerful today. Not only does its language build vocabulary for all ages learning
to read or to speak English, but it lends itself beautifully to being read aloud. Loved it!
I want to sample some more books by this fine author and her illustrator.*

—MARY ANN LeBEAU, MEd, Second-Grade Teacher, NJ

*This delightful retelling of a classic story will intrigue and entertain readers in
second and third grades, as well as English-language learners of any age.*

—VIVIAN JONES SCHMIDT, MEd, 35 years teaching, Charlottesville, VA

*The richness of the story is rivaled by the vibrancy of the colors and images.
It is a genuinely healing story while also offering a powerful tool to build up literacy.
The Shoemaker and the Elves offers a true balm for any young reader
and for any middle-school, high-school, college, or adult learner of English
as a Second Language, all of whom would enjoy it. Thank you so, Ms. Covington,
for this gift to the world, especially in these times!*

—IDA OBERMAN, PhD, Founder and Director, Community School for Creative Education,
a public Charter Waldorf School, Oakland, CA